50 Super Awesome Summer Zucchini Recipes

© Copyright 2016. Laura Sommers.
All rights reserved.
No part of this book may be reproduced in any form or by any electronic or mechanical means without written permission of the author. All text, illustrations and design are the exclusive property of
Laura Sommers
PO Box 33
Phoenix, Maryland 21131

Dedicated to my family.

Introduction 1
Grilled Summer Zucchini 2
Italian Grilled Summer Zucchini 3
Summer Zucchini Pizza 4
Baked Summer Zucchini Chips 5
Summer Zucchini Bake 6
Summer Zucchini Couscous 7
Summer Zucchini Bread 8
Summer Zucchini Pancakes 9
Summer Zucchini Pie 10
Summer Zucchini Pickles 11
Creamy Summer Zucchini Soup 13
Summer Zucchini Kabobs 14
Summer Zucchini Parmesan 15
Summer Zucchini Rice 16
Stuffed Summer Zucchini 17
Summer Zucchini Burritos 18
Summer Zucchini Quiche Recipe 19
Summer Zucchini Casserole Recipe 20
Summer Zucchini Cornbread Recipe 21
Summer Zucchini Stuffing 22
Baked Summer Zucchini Fries 23
Mac and Cheese Summer Zucchini 24
Summer Zucchini Frittata 25
Summer Zucchini Soufflé 26
Summer Zucchini Cakes 27

Summer Zucchini Linguine	28
Summer Zucchini Sauté	29
Summer Zucchini and Eggs	30
Steamed Summer Zucchini	31
Summer Zucchini Brownie	32
Summer Zucchini Muffins	33
Asian Style Summer Zucchini	34
Summer Zucchini Fitters	35
Summer Zucchini Stew	36
Summer Zucchini Curry Soup	37
Summer Zucchini Gazpacho	38
Summer Zucchini Stir Fry	39
Marinated Summer Zucchini	40
Summer Zucchini Leek Pho	41
Summer Zucchini Potato Soup	42
Summer Zucchini Butter	43
Summer Zucchini Boats	44
Summer Zucchini Chocolate Cake	45
Summer Zucchini Burgers	47
Summer Zucchini Salad	48
Summer Zucchini Quesadillas	49
Cajun Summer Zucchini	50
Summer Zucchini Couscous	51
Summer Zucchini Chicken and Prosciutto	52
Summer Zucchini Hummus	53
About the Author	55
Other books by Laura Sommers	56

Introduction

50 Delicious Summer Zucchini Recipes!

Summertime is here and you've worked all Spring on your vegetable garden to get a bountiful harvest of fresh tasty Summer Zucchini. Now all you need are some delicious mouth-watering recipes to impress your friends and family? Look no further. I have created a list of tasty, mouth-watering zucchini recipes. They are simple and easy to prepare. Perfect to take to a party or a pot-luck at work.

This recipe book includes 50 zucchini recipes for you to make for dinner, barbecues, pool parties or get-togethers. Enjoy!

Grilled Summer Zucchini

Ingredients:

2 zucchinis, quartered lengthwise
2 tsps. olive oil
1/2 tsp. garlic powder
1 tsp. Italian seasoning
1 pinch salt
2 tbsps. balsamic vinegar

Directions:

1. Preheat grill for medium-low heat and lightly oil the grate.
2. Brush zucchini with olive oil.
3. Sprinkle garlic powder, Italian seasoning, and salt over zucchini.
4. Cook on preheated grill until beginning to brown, 3-4 minutes per side.
5. Brush balsamic vinegar over the zucchini and continue cooking 1 minute more.
6. Serve and enjoy!

Italian Grilled Summer Zucchini

Ingredients:

1 (8 oz.) bottle Italian salad dressing
2 zucchinis, cut into thick rounds
Salt and ground black pepper to taste

Directions:

1. Pour Italian salad dressing into a resealable plastic bag. Add the zucchini and coat with the dressing. Season generously with salt and black pepper. Squeeze excess air from the bag and seal. Marinate in the refrigerator 30 to 60 minutes.
2. Preheat an outdoor grill for medium-high heat and lightly oil the grate.
3. Remove zucchini from bag; discard dressing.
4. Cook zucchini rounds on preheated grill until lightly browned and soft in the center, 7 to 10 minutes.
5. Serve and enjoy!

Summer Zucchini Pizza

Ingredients:

1 large zucchini
1/2 cup butter, melted
3 cloves crushed garlic
1/2 cup mozzarella cheese
1/2 (14 oz.) can pizza sauce

Directions:

1. Slice the Zucchini into thick rounds.
2. Combine the melted butter and crushed garlic in a small bowl.
3. Set aside.
4. When the coals on your barbeque are almost burned down, lay your zucchini slices on the grill. Let cook for three minutes then turn over and brush the butter/garlic mixture on each slice. Cook for three more minutes and turn over again and brush the other side with the garlic and butter.
5. Cover the slices with pizza sauce and cheese and let cook until the cheese begins to melt.
6. Serve and enjoy!

Baked Summer Zucchini Chips

Ingredients:

1/2 cup panko (Japanese breadcrumbs)
1/4 cup loosely packed fresh basil leaves
1/4 tsp. kosher salt
1/4 cup finely grated Parmesan cheese
1/2 pound zucchini, cut into 1/4-inch-thick rounds
1 tbsp. olive oil
Vegetable cooking spray

Directions:

1. Preheat oven to 450 degrees F.
2. Process first 3 ingredients in a food processor 10 to 15 seconds or until finely ground. Stir together breadcrumb mixture and cheese in a medium bowl.
3. Toss zucchini rounds with oil. Dredge zucchini, 1 round at time, in breadcrumb mixture, pressing gently to adhere.
4. Place rounds in a single layer in a jelly-roll pan coated with cooking spray. Bake 30 minutes or until browned and crisp.
5. Serve and enjoy!

Summer Zucchini Bake

Ingredients:

Cooking spray
1 pound sliced zucchini
1 1/2 cups fresh or frozen corn kernels
1 1/4 pounds sliced vine-ripened tomatoes
1/2 cup panko
1/4 cup finely grated Parmesan

Directions:

1. Preheat oven to 400 degrees F.
2. Coat a 2-quart shallow baking dish with cooking spray, and alternately layer sliced zucchini, corn kernels, and sliced tomatoes.
3. Combine panko and Parmesan, and sprinkle on top. Bake, uncovered, in the center of oven 30 minutes or until top is golden brown.
4. Cover with foil, and bake for 10 minutes more or until vegetables are tender.
5. Serve and enjoy!

Summer Zucchini Couscous

Ingredients:

1 1/2 cups uncooked plain instant couscous
2 cups zucchini, thinly sliced
1 tbsp. lemon juice
1 tsp. kosher salt
3 tbsps. olive oil
1 med. tomato, chopped
1/3 cup chopped fresh mint
1/2 cup golden raisins

Directions:

1. Place instant couscous in a large bowl and add 2 cups boiling water.
2. Cover with plastic wrap and set aside for 5 minutes. Uncover and fluff with a fork. Add lemon juice, kosher salt, olive oil, zucchini, tomato, fresh mint, raisins.
3. Toss until well combined.
4. Serve and enjoy!

Summer Zucchini Bread

Ingredients:

3 cups all-purpose flour
1 tsp. salt
1 tsp. baking soda
1 tsp. baking powder
3 tsps. ground cinnamon
3 eggs
1 cup vegetable oil
2 1/4 cups white sugar
3 tsps. vanilla extract
2 cups grated zucchini
1 cup chopped walnuts

Directions:

1. Grease and flour two 8 x 4 inch pans. Preheat oven to 325 degrees F (165 degrees C).
2. Sift flour, salt, baking powder, soda, and cinnamon together in a bowl.
3. Beat eggs, oil, vanilla, and sugar together in a large bowl.
4. Add sifted ingredients to the creamed mixture, and beat well. Stir in zucchini and nuts until well combined. Pour batter into prepared pans.
5. Bake for 40 to 60 minutes, or until tester inserted in the center comes out clean.
6. Cool in pan on rack for 20 minutes.
7. Remove bread from pan, and let cool.
8. Serve and enjoy!

Summer Zucchini Pancakes

Ingredients:

2 cups grated zucchini
2 large eggs, slightly beaten
2 tbsps. chopped green onion
1/2 cup all-purpose flour
1/4 cup grated Parmesan cheese
1/2 tsp. baking powder
1/2 tsp. salt
1 pinch dried oregano
1/4 cup vegetable oil, or as needed

Directions:

1. Blot grated zucchini with paper towels to remove moisture.
2. Stir zucchini, eggs, and onion in a large bowl. Mix flour, Parmesan cheese, baking powder, salt, and oregano in a separate bowl; stir mixture into zucchini until batter is just moistened.
3. Heat vegetable oil in a large skillet over medium-high heat.
4. Drop rounded spoonfuls of zucchini batter into hot oil; pan fry until golden, 2 to 3 minutes per side.
5. Drain pancakes on a paper towel-lined plate.
6. Serve and enjoy!

Summer Zucchini Pie

Ingredients:

1 (8 oz.) package refrigerated crescent rolls
1/4 cup margarine
4 cups sliced zucchini
1/4 cup chopped onion
2 tbsps. dried parsley
1/4 tsp. dried oregano
1/2 tsp. salt
1/2 tsp. ground black pepper
2 eggs, lightly beaten
2 cups shredded mozzarella cheese

Directions:

1. Preheat oven to 375 degrees F (190 degrees C). Unroll crescent rolls, and press into a 9 inch pie pan, covering sides and bottom.
2. Melt margarine in a skillet over medium heat, and cook the zucchini and onion until tender. Season with parsley, oregano, salt, and pepper. Remove skillet form heat, and mix in the eggs and cheese.
3. Bake 20 minutes in the preheated oven, until set.
4. Let cool.
5. Serve and enjoy!

Summer Zucchini Pickles

Ingredients:

2 pounds zucchini, thinly sliced
1/2 pound onions, quartered and thinly sliced
1/4 cup salt
2 cups white sugar
2 cups apple cider vinegar
1 tsp. celery seed
1 tsp. ground turmeric
1 tsp. prepared yellow mustard
2 tsps. mustard seeds
3 1-quart canning jars with lids and rings

Directions:

1. Place zucchini and onions into a large bowl, cover with water, and stir in salt until dissolved.
2. Let the vegetables soak in the salted water for at least 2 hours; drain and transfer to a large heat proof bowl.
3. Bring sugar, vinegar, celery seed, turmeric, mustard, and mustard seeds to a boil in a saucepan.
4. Pour the mixture over the zucchini and onions.
5. Let the mixture stand for at least 2 more hours.
6. Return zucchini, onions, and pickling liquid with spices to a large pot and bring to a boil and boil for 3 minutes.
7. Sterilize jars and lids in boiling water for at least 5 minutes.
8. Pack the zucchini and onion into the hot, sterilized jars, filling the jars to within 1/4 inch of the top with pickling liquid.
9. Run a knife around the insides of the jars after they have been filled to remove any air bubbles.
10. Wipe the rims of the jars with a moist paper towel to remove any food residue.
11. Top with lids and screw on rings.
12. Place a rack in the bottom of a large stockpot and fill halfway with water.
13. Bring to a boil and lower jars into the boiling water using a holder.
14. Leave a 2-inch space between the jars.
15. Pour in more boiling water if necessary to bring the water level to at least 1 inch above the tops of the jars.
16. Bring the water to a rolling boil, cover the pot, and process for 10 minutes.
17. Remove the jars from the stockpot and place onto a cloth-covered or wood surface, several inches apart, until cool.
18. Once cool, press the top of each lid with a finger, ensuring that the seal is tight.
19. Store in a cool, dark area, and wait at least 24 hours before opening.
20. Serve and enjoy!

Creamy Summer Zucchini Soup

Ingredients:

4 cups shredded zucchini
3/4 cup water
3/4 tsp. salt
1/2 tsp. basil
2 cups warm milk
3 tbsps. all-purpose flour
1/2 tsp. salt
3 tbsps. butter
2 tbsps. minced onion
Ground black pepper to taste

Directions:

1. Stir zucchini, water, salt, and basil together in a pot; bring to a boil, reduce heat to medium-low, and simmer until zucchini is tender, about 15 minutes.
2. Pour zucchini mixture into a blender no more than half full.
3. Cover and hold lid down; pulse a few times before leaving on to blend until smooth.
4. Whisk warm milk, flour, and salt together in a bowl until smooth.
5. Melt butter in a skillet over medium heat. Cook and stir onion in melted butter until translucent, 5 to 7 minutes.
6. Pour pureed zucchini and milk mixture into the skillet.
7. Bring to a boil while stirring continually.
8. Season with pepper.
9. Serve and enjoy!

Summer Zucchini Kabobs

Ingredients:

4 cloves garlic, coarsely chopped
1/2 tsp. salt
1/2 cup fresh orange juice
3 tbsps. fresh lime juice
2 tbsps. olive oil
1/2 tsp. cumin
1/2 tsp. dried oregano

Skewers:

1 (16 oz.) sirloin steak (1 inch thick), cut into 1 1/4-inch pieces
8 (12-inch) wooden skewers, soaked in water 30 minutes
1/2 tsp. salt
1/4 tsp. black pepper
2 med. zucchini, cut on a long diagonal into 1/2-inch-thick slices
2 tbsps. olive oil

Directions:

1. Mash garlic to a paste with salt, then whisk together with orange juice, lime juice, olive oil, cumin and oregano in a bowl.
2. Preheat an outdoor grill to medium-high heat.
3. Thread beef on 4 skewers, leaving a little space between each piece.
4. Put skewers on a baking sheet and sprinkle all over with salt and pepper.
5. Thread zucchini onto 4 skewers so slices can grill cut sides down, then transfer to baking sheet.
6. Lightly brush beef and zucchini all over with oil.
7. Lightly oil grate and grill beef, covered with lid, turning once, about 4 minutes total for medium rare.
8. Transfer to a serving platter.
9. Lightly oil grate again and grill zucchini, covered with lid, turning once, until grill marks appear and zucchini is just tender, 4 to 5 minutes total.
10. Transfer skewers to a serving platter.
11. Drizzle beef and zucchini with about half of sauce, and serve remaining sauce on the side.
12. Serve and enjoy!

Summer Zucchini Parmesan

Ingredients:

2 med. zucchini, peeled and sliced
2 eggs, beaten
2 cups dry Italian seasoned breadcrumbs
8 oz. shredded mozzarella cheese
1/2 cup shredded parmesan cheese
3 -4 cups of your favorite marinara sauce
Olive oil

Directions:

1. Preheat oven to 425 degrees F.
2. Dip zucchini slices in egg and then coat with breadcrumb mixture.
3. Bake on cookie sheets drizzled with olive oil until golden brown, approximately 10 minutes on each side.
4. Reduce oven to 375 degrees F.
5. Spread a thin layer of marinara sauce on the bottom of a 9x9 inch baking dish.
6. Put one layer of breaded zucchini slices on top and coat with more sauce and a generous sprinkling of both cheeses.
7. Repeat this procedure to use up all the zucchini.
8. Cover with tin foil and bake approximately 30 minutes or until top layer of cheese is melted.
9. Serve and enjoy!

Summer Zucchini Rice

Ingredients:

2 cups chicken broth
1 cup long grain rice
1 Tbsp. butter
¼ tsp. garlic powder
1 cup cheddar cheese, shredded
1 zucchini, grated

Directions:

1. In a saucepan add chicken broth, butter, and rice.
2. Bring to a boil.
3. Cover and reduce heat to medium.
4. Cook for 20 minutes or until liquid is absorbed and rice is tender.
5. Do not stir the rice while it's cooking. Only remove the lid to check for doneness at the end of cooking time.
6. When rice is done, remove from heat.
7. Fluff rice.
8. Stir in garlic powder, cheese, and zucchini.
9. Serve and enjoy!

Stuffed Summer Zucchini

Ingredients:

2 zucchini, ends trimmed
3 tbsps. olive oil
2 links Italian-style chicken sausage, casings removed
2 tsps. crushed red pepper flakes (optional)
Salt and pepper to taste
1/2 sweet onion, chopped
3 cloves garlic, chopped
1 (14.5 oz.) can whole peeled tomatoes, drained and chopped
1/2 cup dry bread crumbs
1/4 cup grated Parmesan cheese
1 tbsp. chopped fresh basil

Directions:

1. Preheat oven to 375 degrees F (190 degrees C).
2. Cut a lengthwise 3/4-inch thick slice from each zucchini.
3. Retain the lengthwise slices.
4. With a spoon, scoop out the flesh, leaving a shell intact all around the zucchini.
5. Discard flesh.
6. Chop up the retained lengthwise slices of zucchini.
7. Heat the olive oil in a skillet over medium heat, and cook the chicken sausage, breaking the meat up as it cooks, until the sausage has begun to brown, about 8 minutes.
8. Sprinkle in the crushed red pepper flakes, and season with salt and black pepper.
9. Stir in the chopped zucchini, onion, and garlic, and cook until the onion is translucent, about 5 minutes.
10. Scrape the sausage mixture into a bowl, and stir in the tomatoes, bread crumbs, Parmesan cheese, and basil until the stuffing is thoroughly combined.
11. Lightly stuff the zucchini boats with the stuffing.
12. Place the zucchini into a baking dish, and bake until thoroughly heated through and beginning to brown on top, about 30 minutes.
13. Serve and enjoy!

Summer Zucchini Burritos

Ingredients:

2 tbsps. olive oil
1/2 onion, chopped
2 cloves garlic, pressed
2 zucchini, shredded
1 large yellow squash, shredded
1/2 red bell pepper, chopped
1 (15 oz.) can black beans, rinsed and drained
1 cup green salsa
1/2 tsp. ground cumin
1/2 tsp. ground cayenne pepper
1 (8 oz.) package Mexican style shredded cheese blend, divided
6 burrito-size flour tortillas
1 (8 oz.) package Mexican style shredded cheese blend

Directions:

1. Preheat oven to 350 degrees F. (175 degrees C).
2. Grease a 9x12-inch baking dish.
3. Heat the olive oil in a large skillet over medium heat, and cook the onion and garlic until the onion is translucent, about 5 minutes.
4. Stir in the zucchini, yellow squash, and red bell pepper.
5. Cook, stirring frequently, until the zucchini and squash are tender, about 10 minutes.
6. Stir in the black beans, green salsa, cumin, and cayenne pepper.
7. Cook and stir the filling until it thickens, 5 to 8 more minutes.
8. Divide one of the packages of Mexican-style cheese among the tortillas.
9. Spoon zucchini-squash filling into each tortilla, over the cheese, in a line down the center.
10. Roll up the tortillas, and place them into the prepared baking dish with the seam sides down.
11. Bake in the preheated oven until the cheese is melted and the tortillas are heated through, about 15 minutes.
12. Sprinkle the other package of shredded cheese over the tortillas.
13. Serve and enjoy!

Summer Zucchini Quiche Recipe

Ingredients:

1/2 (14.1-oz.) package refrigerated pie dough
1 tbsp. olive oil
4 cups (1/8-inch-thick) slices zucchini
3 garlic cloves, minced
3/4 tsp. kosher salt, divided
1/2 cup finely chopped Basic Caramelized Onions
1 cup 1% low-fat milk
1 1/2 tbsps. all-purpose flour
1/2 tsp. freshly ground black pepper
3 large eggs
½ cup grated Parmigiano-Reggiano cheese

Directions:

1. Preheat oven to 425 degrees F.
2. Roll dough into a 12-inch circle.
3. Fit dough into a 10-inch deep-dish pie plate.
4. Fold edges under and flute.
5. Line dough with foil.
6. Bake for 12 minutes or until edges are golden.
7. Remove foil and bake an additional 2 minutes.
8. Cool on a wire rack.
9. Reduce oven temperature to 375 degrees F.
10. Heat a large nonstick skillet over medium-high heat.
11. Add oil to pan; swirl.
12. Add zucchini and garlic; sprinkle with 1/4 teaspoon salt.
13. Sauté 5 minutes or until crisp-tender.
14. Cool slightly.
15. Arrange Basic Caramelized Onions over bottom of crust.
16. Top with zucchini mixture.
17. Combine remaining 1/2 teaspoon salt, milk, flour, pepper, eggs, and cheese in a medium bowl, stirring well with a whisk.
18. Pour milk mixture over zucchini mixture.
19. Bake for 35 minutes.
20. Serve and enjoy!

Summer Zucchini Casserole Recipe

Ingredients:

1 1/2 cups grated Cheddar cheese
1/3 cup grated Parmesan cheese
1/2 tsp. dried oregano
1/2 tsp. dried basil
2 cloves garlic, minced
salt and pepper to taste
2 med. zucchinis, thinly sliced
5 plum tomatoes, thinly sliced
1/4 cup butter
2 tbsps. finely chopped onion
3/4 cup fine bread crumbs

Directions:

1. Preheat oven to 375 degrees F (190 degrees C).
2. Lightly butter a 9x9-inch pan.
3. In a large bowl, combine Cheddar, Parmesan, oregano, basil, and garlic. Season with salt and pepper, and set aside.
4. Arrange half of the zucchini slices in the pan. Sprinkle 1/4 of the cheese and herb mixture on top. Arrange half of the tomatoes, and top with another 1/4 of the cheese mixture. Repeat layers.
5. Melt butter in a skillet over medium heat. Stir in onions, and cook until soft and translucent.
6. Stir in breadcrumbs; cook until they have absorbed the butter. Sprinkle on top of casserole.
7. Cover loosely with foil, and bake in a preheated oven for 25 minutes. Remove foil, and bake until the top is crusty and the vegetables are tender, about 20 minutes.
8. Serve and enjoy!

Summer Zucchini Cornbread Recipe

Ingredients:

1 cup coarsely chopped zucchini
1 cup milk
1/2 cup chopped onion
2 eggs
1/4 cup vegetable oil
1 1/4 cups cornmeal
1 cup all-purpose flour
2 tbsps. white sugar
4 tsps. baking powder
1 tsp. salt
1 cup shredded Cheddar cheese

Directions:

1. Preheat oven to 400 degrees F (200 degrees C).
2. Grease a 10-inch cast-iron skillet, and place it into the oven while it preheats.
3. Place the zucchini, milk, onion, eggs, and vegetable oil into a blender, and pulse 5 to 8 times, until thoroughly mixed and the zucchini and onion have been chopped into very small pieces.
4. Mix together the cornmeal, flour, sugar, baking powder, and salt in a large bowl. Pour the zucchini mixture into the cornmeal mixture, stirring to combine, and gently mix in the Cheddar cheese.
5. Carefully pour the batter into the hot greased skillet, smooth it out with a spoon, and bake until the cornbread is golden brown and a toothpick inserted into the center comes out clean, about 30 minutes.
6. Serve and enjoy!

Summer Zucchini Stuffing

Ingredients:

1 tbsp. vegetable oil
2 cups grated zucchini
1 med. onion, minced
5 cups cornbread crumbs
2 cups sourdough bread crumbs
1 cup chicken broth
1/2 cup sour cream
1/2 cup butter, melted
2 eggs
1 tsp. dried sage
1/2 tsp. poultry seasoning
1/2 tsp. salt
1/2 tsp. ground black pepper

Directions:

1. Preheat oven to 375 degrees F (190 degrees C).
2. Lightly oil a 9x13-inch baking dish.
3. Heat 1 tablespoon oil in skillet over medium heat.
4. Add zucchini and onion; saute until zucchini is softened slightly, about 3 minutes.
5. Remove from heat.
6. In large bowl, combine cornbread and sourdough crumbs, chicken broth, sour cream, and butter. Stir in zucchini mixture, eggs, sage, poultry seasoning, salt, and pepper. Mix until evenly moistened. Spread into prepared baking dish.
7. Bake in preheated oven until lightly browned, 30 to 40 minutes.
8. Serve and enjoy!

Baked Summer Zucchini Fries

Ingredients:

cooking spray
1/2 cup bread crumbs
1/4 cup grated Parmesan cheese
2 eggs, beaten
3 zucchinis, ends trimmed, halved, and cut into 1/2-inch strips

Directions:

1. Preheat oven to 425 degrees F (220 degrees C).
2. Line a baking sheet with aluminum foil and spray with cooking spray.
3. Stir bread crumbs and Parmesan cheese together in a shallow bowl. Whisk eggs in a separate shallow bowl.
4. Working in batches, dip zucchini strips into egg mixture, shake to remove any excess, and roll strips in bread crumb mixture to coat. Transfer coated zucchini strips to the prepared baking sheet.
5. Bake zucchini fries in the preheated oven, turning once, until golden and crisp, 20 to 24 minutes.
6. Serve and enjoy!

Mac and Cheese Summer Zucchini

Ingredients:

1 med. zucchini, sliced thinly
1/4 cup butter
1/4 cup flour
1/2 tsp. salt
1/2 tsp. oregano
1/4 tsp. garlic salt
2 cup milk
2 cup (8 oz.) shredded sharp Cheddar cheese
2 cup (7 oz.) elbow macaroni, cooked
1/2 cup tomato, chopped

Directions:

1. Sauté zucchini in butter; blend in flour and seasoning.
2. Gradually add milk; cook, stirring constantly, until thickened.
3. Add 1 1/2 cups cheese.
4. Stir until melted.
5. Stir in macaroni and tomato and pour into a 1 1/2 quart casserole.
6. Bake at 350 degrees for at least 15 minutes.
7. Top with remaining cheese and continue baking until cheese is melted.
8. Serve and enjoy!

Summer Zucchini Frittata

Ingredients:

1 cup water
3 tbsps. olive oil
1/2 tsp. salt
1/2 green bell pepper, seeded and chopped
3 zucchini, cut into 1/2-inch slices
2 cloves garlic, peeled
1 small onion, diced
6 fresh chopped mushrooms
1 tbsp. butter
5 eggs
Salt and pepper to taste
1 cup shredded mozzarella cheese
3 tbsps. Parmesan cheese

Directions:

1. Preheat oven to 350 degrees F (175 degrees C).
2. In a large skillet or sauce pan, combine water, olive oil, salt, green pepper, zucchini and garlic cloves.
3. Simmer until zucchini is tender, about 5 to 7 minutes.
4. Drain off water and discard garlic.
5. Stir in onion, mushrooms and butter.
6. Cook until onion is transparent.
7. Add eggs and stir; season with salt and pepper.
8. Cook over low heat until eggs are firm.
9. Sprinkle mozzarella cheese over eggs.
10. Bake for 10 minutes.
11. Remove from oven and sprinkle with Parmesan cheese.
12. Place under broiler for 5 minutes.
13. Let stand 5 minutes.
14. Serve and enjoy!

Summer Zucchini Soufflé

Ingredients:

1 cup flour
1 tsp. baking powder
4 eggs
1/2 cup vegetable oil
1 onion, chopped
2 pounds zucchini, peeled and diced
Salt and pepper to taste
Paprika
Chopped fresh parsley

Directions:

1. Preheat the oven to 350 degrees F (175 degrees C).
2. Sift flour and baking powder together into a bowl.
3. Lightly beat eggs, and mix them into the flour with the oil.
4. Stir in the onion and zucchini, and season with salt and pepper.
5. Pour mixture into a well-greased 9x13 inch baking dish, and sprinkle with paprika and parsley.
6. Bake for one hour.
7. Serve and enjoy!

Summer Zucchini Cakes

Ingredients:

2 cups shredded zucchini
1 cup Italian seasoned bread crumbs
1 egg
1 tbsp. mayonnaise
1 tsp. prepared mustard
1 tbsp. Old Bay seasoning

Directions:

1. Preheat oven to 350 degrees F (175 degrees C).
2. Grease a baking sheet.
3. In a large bowl combine zucchini, bread crumbs, egg, mayonnaise, mustard and Old Bay Seasoning.
4. Mix well and form into patties.
5. Place on prepared baking sheet.
6. Bake for 20 minutes and turn patties.
7. Bake for another 20 minutes, or until golden brown.
8. Serve and enjoy!

Summer Zucchini Linguine

Ingredients:

1 (8 oz.) package linguine pasta
1 tbsp. olive oil
2 cloves garlic, minced
3 zucchini, shredded
1/4 cup shredded Cheddar cheese
1/4 cup plain nonfat yogurt
Salt and pepper to taste

Directions:

1. Bring a large pot of lightly salted water to a boil.
2. Add pasta and cook for 8 to 10 minutes or until al dente; drain.
3. Meanwhile, heat oil in a large skillet over medium heat.
4. Sauté garlic until it starts to brown.
5. Stir in a handful of grated zucchini; cook for 1 minute and then add the rest of the zucchini.
6. Cook for 3 minutes.
7. Toss pasta with zucchini, cheese and yogurt.
8. Season with salt and pepper. Mix well and serve.
9. Serve and enjoy!

Summer Zucchini Sauté

Ingredients:

3 tbsps. butter
1/3 cup chopped pecans
1 pound fresh zucchini, sliced
1 tbsp. grated Parmesan cheese

Directions:

1. In a large skillet, melt 1 tablespoon butter over medium heat.
2. Add pecans; cook and stir until lightly browned, about 5 minutes.
3. Remove pecans from skillet.
4. Add remaining 2 tablespoons butter to the skillet, and melt.
5. Add zucchini, and sauté until soft.
6. Toss with pecans and cheese.
7. Serve and enjoy!

Summer Zucchini and Eggs

Ingredients:

2 tsps. olive oil
1 small zucchini, sliced
1 egg, beaten
salt and pepper to taste

Directions:

1. Heat a small skillet over medium heat.
2. Pour in oil and sauté zucchini until tender.
3. Spread out zucchini in an even layer, and pour beaten egg evenly over top.
4. Cook until egg is firm.
5. Season with salt and pepper to taste.
6. Serve and enjoy!

Steamed Summer Zucchini

Ingredients:

4 zucchini
2 cloves garlic
1 tbsp. olive oil

Directions:

1. Bring a large pot of water to a boil.
2. Trim ends from zucchini.
3. Cut each one in half, then cut each half lengthwise into quarters.
4. Place zucchini and garlic into a steamer basket, then place the steamer basket into the pot.
5. Steam for 10 to 15 minutes, or until the zucchini are tender.
6. Transfer zucchini to a large bowl.
7. Mash the garlic and put it in the bowl with the zucchini.
8. Drizzle the olive oil into the bowl and toss until the vegetables are coated with oil and garlic.
9. Serve and enjoy!

Summer Zucchini Brownie

Ingredients:

1/2 cup applesauce
2 bananas mashed
1 1/2 cup sugar
2 tsp. vanilla extract
1/2 cup cocoa powder
1 1/2 tsp. baking soda
1/2 tsp salt
2 cups finely shredded zucchini
2 cups all-purpose flour
1/2 cup walnut pieces

Directions:

1. Preheat oven to 350 degrees F.
2. Grease and flour a 9x13 inch baking pan.
3. In a large bowl, mix together the applesauce, mashed bananas and sugar.
4. Add vanilla and cocoa and mix together.
5. Add baking soda, salt, and zucchini and mix together.
6. Add flour and walnuts and mix together.
7. Spread evenly into a prepared pan.
8. Bake for 25 minutes until brownies spring back when gently touched.
9. Serve and enjoy!

Summer Zucchini Muffins

Ingredients:

1 1/2 cup zucchini, grated
1 1/2 cup rolled oats (not instant)
1 1/2 cup whole wheat flour
2 t baking soda
2 t cream of tartar
1 1/2 tsp. cinnamon
1/4 tsp. nutmeg
1/2 cup honey
1/4 cup pineapple juice concentrate
1 t vanilla
3/4 cup applesauce, unsweetened
8 oz. crushed pineapple, drained
2 egg whites
6 dried apricots, finely chopped
1/4 cup pecans, chopped
2 T flax meal

Directions:

1. Preheat oven to 325 degrees F.
2. Coat two muffin pans with nonstick cooking spray.
3. Grate zucchini and place in paper towels or cotton cloth; squeeze to remove moisture. In a mixing bowl combine oats, flour, baking soda, cream of tartar, and spices.
4. In a separate bowl combine honey, applesauce, drained pineapple, apricots, vanilla, and pineapple juice. Stir in egg whites.
5. Combine the wet mixture with the dry; stir only until combined.
6. Portion out 18 muffins in the prepared tins.
7. Combine pecans with flax meal.
8. Top each muffin with 1/2 teaspoon of mixture.
9. Bake for 20 minutes.
10. Serve and enjoy!

Asian Style Summer Zucchini

Ingredients:

1 teaspoon butter
1 large zucchini, halved lengthwise and cut into 1 inch slices
2 tbsps. soy sauce, divided
2 tbsps. sesame seeds
Garlic powder to taste
Ground black pepper to taste

Directions:

1. Melt the butter in a skillet over medium heat.
2. Stir in the zucchini, and cook until lightly browned.
3. Sprinkle with soy sauce and sesame seeds.
4. Season with garlic powder and pepper, and continue cooking until zucchini is well coated and tender.
5. Serve and enjoy!

Summer Zucchini Fitters

Ingredients:

1 1/2 pounds zucchini, grated
1 tsp. salt
1/4 cup all-purpose flour
1/4 cup grated Parmesan cheese
1 large egg, beaten
2 cloves garlic, minced
Kosher salt and ground black pepper to taste
2 tbsps. olive oil

Directions:

1. Toss zucchini and salt together in a large colander and place in sink to drain for 10 minutes.
2. Put zucchini in the middle of a piece of cheesecloth; wrap cheesecloth around zucchini and squeeze to drain as much moisture from zucchini as possible.
3. Mix flour, Parmesan cheese, egg, garlic, kosher salt, and pepper together in a large bowl.
4. Stir in zucchini.
5. Heat olive oil in a large skillet over medium-high heat.
6. Scoop batter by the tablespoon into the hot skillet and fry until golden brown, about 2 minutes per side.
7. Serve and enjoy!

Summer Zucchini Stew

Ingredients:

1 tbsp. olive oil
2 Italian sausages, sliced
1 med. onion, finely diced
1 large potato, diced
1 med. green bell pepper, sliced
2 cloves garlic, minced
1 large zucchini, diced
1 (28 oz.) can roma tomatoes, with juice
2 ½ cups water
1 tbsp. chopped fresh basil
1 tsp. dried oregano
1 tsp. chopped fresh parsley
Salt and pepper to taste
1 (15 oz.) can green beans, drained

Directions:

1. Heat the olive oil in a large pot over medium heat.
2. Mix in the sausages, onion, potato, green bell pepper, and garlic.
3. Cook 10 minutes, stirring often, until potatoes are slightly tender.
4. Mix the zucchini into pot.
5. Add tomatoes and water.
6. Season with basil, oregano, parsley, salt, and pepper.
7. Bring to a boil, reduce to low, and simmer 40 minutes.
8. Stir the green beans into the pot, and continue cooking 5 minutes, until beans are heated through.
9. Serve and enjoy!

Summer Zucchini Curry Soup

Ingredients:

2 tbsps. extra virgin olive oil
1 large onion, halved and thinly sliced
1 tbsp. curry powder
sea salt to taste
4 small zucchini, halved lengthwise and cut into 1 inch slices
1 quart chicken stock

Directions:

1. Heat the oil in a large pot.
2. Stir in the onion, and season with curry powder and salt.
3. Cook and stir until onion is tender.
4. Stir in zucchini, and cook until tender.
5. Pour in the chicken stock. Bring to a boil. Cover, reduce heat to low, and simmer 20 minutes.
6. Remove soup from heat.
7. Blend until almost smooth using a hand blender.
8. Serve and enjoy!

Summer Zucchini Gazpacho

Ingredients:

2 cups shredded zucchini
1 onion, coarsely chopped
1 avocado, peeled, pitted, and coarsely chopped
1/2 cup canned garbanzo beans, drained
1/4 cup apple cider vinegar
1 jalapeno pepper, seeded and minced
2 tsps. lemon juice
1 clove garlic, smashed
1/4 tsp. salt
1/4 tsp. ground black pepper

Directions:

1. Combine zucchini, onion, avocado, garbanzo beans, apple cider vinegar, jalapeno pepper, lemon juice, garlic, salt, and pepper together in a bowl.
2. Chill in refrigerator for at least 1 hour.
3. Serve and enjoy!

Summer Zucchini Stir Fry

Ingredients:

1/3 cup broccoli florets
1/3 cup cauliflower florets
1/2 cup shelled edamame
1 large carrot, chopped
1 tbsp. water
2 tbsps. olive oil
1 onion, chopped
1 zucchini, sliced
5 large mushrooms, sliced
1 tbsp. finely chopped garlic
1 1/2 tbsps. teriyaki sauce
2 tbsps. agave nectar

Directions:

1. Combine broccoli, cauliflower, edamame, carrots, and water in a microwave-safe bowl.
2. Cover with plastic wrap and microwave for 1 minute until vegetables are tender.
3. Set aside.
4. Heat olive oil in a skillet over medium heat; add onion.
5. Cook and stir until onion is softened and beginning to brown, about 10 minutes.
6. Stir cooked broccoli, cauliflower, edamame, carrots, zucchini, mushrooms, and garlic into the pan.
7. Cook and stir until vegetables are cooked through, about 5 minutes.
8. Stir in reduced-sodium teriyaki sauce and agave nectar.
9. Cook 5 more minutes.
10. Serve and enjoy!

Marinated Summer Zucchini

Ingredients:

1/4 cup olive oil
3 large zucchini, thinly sliced
2 cloves garlic, minced
2 cups fresh mint leaves, finely chopped
1/3 cup distilled white vinegar
1/2 tsp. salt
Ground black pepper to taste
1 tbsp. olive oil, for drizzling

Directions:

1. Heat 1/4 cup of olive oil in a large skillet over medium-high heat.
2. Add zucchini slices and garlic.
3. Cook and stir until starting to brown but you want the squash to stay firm and not get mushy, 3 to 4 minutes.
4. Remove from the heat and mix in the vinegar, mint, salt and pepper. Stir in the remaining olive oil.
5. Spoon into a jar and store covered in the refrigerator.
6. Serve and enjoy!

Summer Zucchini Leek Pho

Ingredients:

2 tbsps. vegetable oil
2 cloves garlic, minced
8 cups chicken broth
3 large carrots, sliced into 1/4-inch pieces
1 tsp. curry powder
1 tsp. ginger powder
1 pinch cayenne pepper, or more to taste
Salt and ground black pepper to taste
2 tbsps. lime juice
2 large zucchini, peeled and cut into noodle shape
1 large leek, sliced into 1/4-inch pieces
3 stalks celery, sliced into 1/4-inch pieces
1 cup sliced fresh mushrooms
1/2 cup chopped cilantro

Directions:

1. Heat oil in a large stockpot over medium-high heat; cook and stir garlic until fragrant and browned, 2 to 3 minutes. Increase heat to high.
2. Add chicken broth and bring to a boil.
3. Add carrots, curry powder, ginger, cayenne pepper, salt, and pepper; cook and stir until carrots are tender, 5 to 7 minutes.
4. Add lime juice.
5. Stir zucchini noodles, leek, celery, and mushrooms into broth; cook, stirring occasionally, until liquid boils again.
6. Reduce heat and simmer until vegetables are tender, about 10 minutes.
7. Pile the zucchini noodles and vegetables into each serving bowl using tongs or pasta forks.
8. Ladle broth over them and top with cilantro.
9. Serve and enjoy!

Summer Zucchini Potato Soup

Ingredients:

5 cups chicken broth
4 small zucchini, diced
1 large potato, diced
1 large onion, chopped
3 eggs
2 tbsps. lemon juice
1 1/2 tsps. dried dill weed
salt and ground black pepper to taste

Directions:

1. Bring broth to a boil in a saucepan; add zucchini, potato, and onion. Reduce heat to medium-low, cover the saucepan, and simmer until vegetables are tender, about 15 minutes.
2. Beat eggs and lemon juice together; add 1/2 cup of the hot broth from the saucepan and beat to temper the eggs. Pour the egg mixture into the broth in the saucepan.
3. Increase heat to medium; cook, stirring constantly, for 1 minute.
4. Remove saucepan from heat, stir dill into the soup, and season with salt and pepper.
5. Serve and enjoy!

Summer Zucchini Butter

Ingredients:

2 pounds zucchini, more or less*
1/4 cup olive oil or butter, if you prefer
2 minced shallots, garlic, or combination of both
Salt and pepper

Directions:

1. Coarsely grate the zucchini. Let it drain in a colander for 3 to 4 minutes or until you are ready to begin cooking. To hasten cooking time, squeeze the water out of the zucchini by wringing it in a clean cloth towel.
2. In a deep skillet, heat the olive oil/butter.
3. Sauté the shallots briefly.
4. Add the zucchini and toss.
5. Cook and stir over medium to medium-high heat until the zucchini reaches a spreadable consistency.
6. Serve and enjoy!

Summer Zucchini Boats

Ingredients:

2 med. zucchini
3/4 pound ground beef
1 small onion, chopped
1/2 cup chopped fresh mushrooms
1/2 cup chopped sweet red pepper
1/2 cup chopped green pepper
1 cup shredded cheddar cheese, divided
2 tbsps. ketchup
Salt and pepper to taste

Directions:

1. Preheat oven to 350 degrees F.
2. Trim the ends off zucchini.
3. Cut zucchini in half lengthwise; scoop out pulp, leaving 1/2-in. shells. Finely chop pulp.
4. In a skillet, cook beef, zucchini pulp, onion, mushrooms and peppers over medium heat until meat is no longer pink; drain.
5. Remove from the heat.
6. Add 1/2 cup cheese, ketchup, salt and pepper; mix well.
7. Spoon into the zucchini shells.
8. Place in a greased 13x9-in. baking dish. Sprinkle with remaining cheese.
9. Bake, uncovered, for 25-30 minutes or until zucchini is tender.
10. Serve and enjoy!

Summer Zucchini Chocolate Cake

Cake Ingredients:

1/2 cup butter, softened
1-1/2 cups sugar
2 large eggs
1/4 cup unsweetened applesauce
1 tsp. vanilla extract
2-1/2 cups all-purpose flour
1/2 cup baking cocoa
1-1/4 tsps. baking powder
1 tsp. salt
1 tsp. ground cinnamon
1/2 tsp. baking soda
1/2 cup fat-free milk
3 cups shredded zucchini
1/2 cup chopped walnuts
1 tbsp. grated orange peel

Glaze Ingredients:

1-1/4 cups confectioners' sugar
2 tbsps. orange juice
1 tsp. vanilla extract

Directions:

1. Preheat oven to 350 degrees F.
2. Coat a 10-in. fluted tube pan with cooking spray and sprinkle with flour.
3. In a large bowl, cream butter and sugar until light and fluffy.
4. Add eggs, one at a time, beating well after each addition.
5. Beat in applesauce and vanilla.
6. Combine the flour, cocoa, baking powder, salt, cinnamon and soda; add to creamed mixture alternately with milk, beating well after each addition. Fold in the zucchini, walnuts and orange peel.
7. Transfer to prepared pan.
8. Bake for 50-60 minutes or until a toothpick inserted near the center comes out clean.
9. Cool for 10 minutes before removing from pan to a wire rack to cool completely.
10. Combine glaze ingredients;

11. Drizzle over cake.
12. Serve and enjoy!

Summer Zucchini Burgers

Ingredients:

2 cups shredded zucchini
1 med. onion, finely chopped
1/2 cup dry bread crumbs
2 large eggs, lightly beaten
1/8 tsp. salt
Dash cayenne pepper
3 hard-cooked large egg whites, chopped
2 tbsps. canola oil
4 whole wheat hamburger buns, split
4 lettuce leaves
4 slices tomato
4 slices onion

Directions:

1. In a sieve or colander, drain zucchini, squeezing to remove excess liquid. Pat dry. In a small bowl, combine the zucchini, onion, bread crumbs, eggs, salt and cayenne.
2. Gently stir in cooked egg whites.
3. Heat 1 tablespoon oil in a large nonstick skillet over medium-low heat.
4. Drop batter by cupfuls into oil.
5. Press lightly to flatten.
6. Fry in batches until golden brown on both sides, using remaining oil as needed.
7. Serve and enjoy!

Summer Zucchini Salad

Ingredients:

7 large heirloom tomatoes (about 2-1/2 pounds), cut into wedges
3 med. zucchini, halved lengthwise and thinly sliced
2 med. sweet yellow peppers, thinly sliced
1/3 cup cider vinegar
3 tbsps. olive oil
1 tbsp. sugar
1-1/2 tsps. salt
1 tbsp. minced fresh basil
1 tbsp. parsley
1 tbsp. tarragon

Directions:

1. In a large bowl, combine tomatoes, zucchini and peppers.
2. In a small bowl, whisk vinegar, oil, sugar and salt until blended.
3. Stir in herbs.
4. Just before serving, drizzle dressing over salad; toss gently to coat.
5. Serve and enjoy!

Summer Zucchini Quesadillas

Ingredients:

2 med. red potatoes, quartered and sliced
1 med. zucchini, quartered and sliced
1 med. sweet red pepper, sliced
1 small onion, chopped
2 tbsps. olive oil
1 garlic clove, minced
1/2 tsp. salt
1/2 tsp. dried oregano
1/4 tsp. pepper
1 cup shredded mozzarella cheese
1 cup shredded cheddar cheese
8 tortillas

Directions:

1. Preheat oven to 425 degrees F.
2. In a large bowl, combine the first nine ingredients.
3. Transfer to a 15-in. x 10-in. x 1-in. baking pan.
4. Bake for 24-28 minutes or until potatoes are tender.
5. In a small bowl, combine cheeses.
6. Place tortillas on a griddle coated with cooking spray.
7. Spread 1/3 cup vegetable mixture over half of each tortilla.
8. Sprinkle with 1/4 cup cheese.
9. Fold over and cook over low heat for 1-2 minutes on each side or until cheese is melted.
10. Serve and enjoy!

Cajun Summer Zucchini

Ingredients:

2 med. yellow summer squash, sliced
2 med. zucchini, sliced
1-3/4 cups sliced fresh mushrooms
1/2 med. onion, sliced and separated into rings
1/2 med. red onion, sliced and separated into rings
1 cup cherry tomatoes
1/4 cup sliced fresh carrots
1 tsp. Cajun seasoning

Directions:

1. Place vegetables in a grill wok or basket.
2. Grill, uncovered, over medium heat for 8-12 minutes or until tender, stirring frequently. Transfer to a large bowl.
3. Sprinkle with Cajun seasoning; toss to coat.
4. Serve and enjoy!

Summer Zucchini Couscous

Ingredients:

1/2 pound mushrooms, quartered
1 med. zucchini, halved lengthwise and cut into 1/4-inch slices
1 med. sweet red pepper, cut into 1-inch pieces
1/4 cup dry red wine or reduced-sodium chicken broth
3 tbsps. Dijon mustard
2 tbsps. olive oil
2 garlic cloves, minced
1 tsp. prepared horseradish
1/2 tsp. salt
1/4 tsp. pepper
1 cup water
1 cup uncooked couscous

Directions:

1. Preheat oven to 350 degrees F.
2. Place an 18x12-in. piece of foil on a large baking sheet and set aside.
3. In a large bowl, combine the mushrooms, zucchini and red pepper.
4. Combine the wine, mustard, oil, garlic, horseradish, salt and pepper; drizzle over vegetables. Toss to coat; transfer to baking sheet.
5. Top with another piece of foil.
6. Bring edges of foil pieces together; crimp to seal, forming a large packet.
7. Bake for 20-25 minutes or until vegetables are tender.
8. Open foil carefully to allow steam to escape.
9. Meanwhile, in a small saucepan, bring water to a boil.
10. Stir in couscous. Remove from the heat; cover and let stand for 5-10 minutes or until water is absorbed.
11. Fluff with a fork.
12. Transfer couscous and vegetables to a large serving bowl.
13. Toss to combine.
14. Serve and enjoy!

Summer Zucchini Chicken and Prosciutto

Ingredients:

4 boneless, skinless chicken breasts
1/2 tsp. kosher salt
1/2 tsp. black pepper
2 tbsps. olive oil
1/4 pound (about 8 slices) prosciutto
3 small zucchini, thinly sliced into half-moons
1 clove garlic, thinly sliced
1 lemon

Directions:

1. Heat oven to 400 degrees F.
2. Season the chicken with ¼ teaspoon each of the salt and pepper.
3. Heat 1 tablespoon of the oil in a large ovenproof skillet over medium-high heat.
4. Cook the chicken for 2 minutes per side.
5. Transfer the chicken to the oven and roast for 8 minutes.
6. Meanwhile, in a second skillet, over medium heat, heat the remaining oil.
7. Cook the prosciutto until crisp, 1 to 2 minutes per side.
8. Transfer to a plate.
9. Add the zucchini, garlic, and remaining salt and pepper to the skillet and cook until tender, about 3 minutes.
10. Add the prosciutto and zucchini mixture to the skillet with the chicken, squeeze the lemon over the top, and toss.
11. Divide among the plates.
12. Serve and enjoy!

Summer Zucchini Hummus

Ingredients:

2 small zucchini, peeled and cut into chunks
2 tablespoons lemon juice
1 tablespoon tahini
1 clove garlic, minced
1/2 teaspoon salt
2 tablespoons olive oil
1 pinch ground cumin
1 pinch paprika

Directions:

1. Blend zucchini, lemon juice, tahini, garlic, and salt in a blender until creamy.
2. Stream olive oil into the hummus while blending until completely incorporated.
3. Continue blending until smooth, 1 to 2 minutes.
4. Transfer to a serving bowl.
5. Sprinkle cumin and paprika over the hummus.
6. Serve and enjoy!

The End

About the Author

Laura Sommers is a loving wife and mother who lives on a small farm in Baltimore County, Maryland and has a passion for all things domestic especially when it comes to saving money. She has a profitable eBay business and is a couponing addict. She challenges herself to write books that are enriching, enjoyable, and often unconventional.

Other books by Laura Sommers

- Easy to Make Party Dip Recipes: Chips and Dips and Salsa and Whips!
- Super Slimming Vegan Soup Recipes!
- Popcorn Lovers Recipe Book
- Inexpensive Low Carb Recipes
- Recipes for the Zombie Apocalypse: Cooking Meals with Shelf Stable Foods
- Best Traditional Irish Recipes for St. Patrick's Day
- Egg Recipes for People With Backyard Chickens
- Awesome Sugar Free Diabetic Pie Recipes
- Super Awesome Traditional Maryland Recipes
- Super Awesome Farm Fresh Pork Chop Recipes

May all of your meals be a banquet
with good friends and good food.

Made in the USA
Thornton, CO
09/04/22 16:45:05

1077a2d8-2510-4beb-a80c-90636bea7b99R02